D1326059

L

A Note to Parents

DK READERS is a compelling programme for beginning readers, designed in conjunction with leading literacy experts, including Dr. Linda Gambrell, Distinguished Professor of Education at Clemson University, South Carolina, USA. Dr. Gambrell has served as President of the National Reading Conference, the College Reading Association, and the International Reading Association.

Beautiful illustrations and superb full-colour photographs combine with engaging, easy-to-read stories to offer a fresh approach to each subject in the series. Each DK READER is guaranteed to capture a child's interest while developing his or her reading skills, general knowledge, and love of reading.

The five levels of DK READERS are aimed at different reading abilities, enabling you to choose the books that are exactly right for your child:

Pre-level 1: Learning to read
Level 1: Beginning to read
Level 2: Beginning to read alone
Level 3: Reading alone
Level 4: Proficient readers

The "normal" age at which a child begins to read can be anywhere from three to eight years old. Adult participation through the lower levels is very helpful for providing encouragement, discussing storylines, and sounding out unfamiliar words.

No matter which level you select, you can be sure that you are helping your child learn to read, then read to learn!

LONDON, NEW YORK, MUNICH,
MELBOURNE, and DELHI

For DK/BradyGames

Title Manager Tim Fitzpatrick
Cover Designer Tim Amrhein
Production Designer Wil Cruz
Vice-president & Publisher Mike Degler
Editor-in-chief H. Leigh Davis
Licensing Manager Christian Sumner
Marketing Manager Katie Hemlock
Digital Publishing Manager Tim Cox
Operations Manager Stacey Beheler
Reading Consultant Linda B. Gambrell, Ph.D.
Anglicisation Scarlett O'Hara

For WWE

Global Publishing Manager Steve Pantaleo
Photo Department Frank Vitucci,
Josh Tottenham, Jamie Nelson, Mike Moran,
JD Sestito, Melissa Halladay, Lea Girard
Legal Lauren Dienes-Middlen

First published in Great Britain in 2014 by
Dorling Kindersley Limited
80 Strand, London, WC2R 0RL

10 9 8 7 6 5 4 3 2 1
001-271946-Oct/2014

Page design copyright © 2014 Dorling Kindersley Limited

A CIP catalogue record for this book is available
from the British Library.

ISBN: 978-0-24100-841-6

Colour reproduction in the UK by Altaimage
Printed and bound in China

The publisher would like to thank the following for their kind
permission to reproduce their photographs:
All photos courtesy WWE Entertainment, Inc.

All other images © Dorling Kindersley
For further information see: www.dkimages.com

Discover more at
www.dk.com

Daniel Bryan

Written by Steve Pantaleo

Few Superstars in history have captured the imagination of the WWE Universe quite like Daniel Bryan. His "Yes! Movement," supported with booming chants of "Yes! Yes! Yes!" is taking over WWE. At *WrestleMania 30*, nearly 80,000 delirious fans rallied behind the Bearded Warrior.

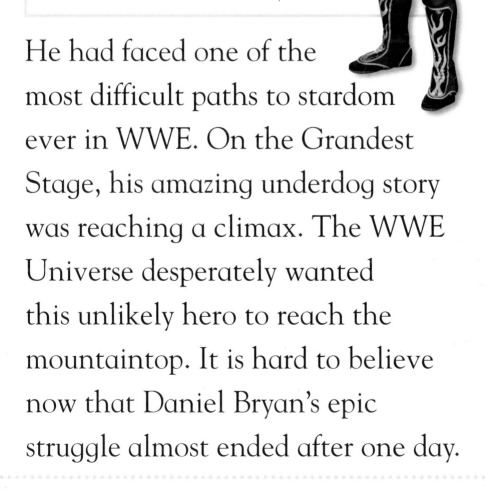

Daniel Bryan Stats

Height: 1.5 m
Weight: 95 kg
Hometown: Aberdeen, WA, USA
Signature Moves: "Yes!" Lock

He had faced one of the most difficult paths to stardom ever in WWE. On the Grandest Stage, his amazing underdog story was reaching a climax. The WWE Universe desperately wanted this unlikely hero to reach the mountaintop. It is hard to believe now that Daniel Bryan's epic struggle almost ended after one day.

Daniel Bryan spent ten years on the independent wrestling scene before being noticed by WWE. Despite being small for a Superstar, he was given a chance to prove himself on the first season of *WWE NXT*. While there, he clashed with his WWE "mentor", The Miz.

In the ring, he lost all his matches and was cast off with a record of 0-10. Still seeking to make an impact, he aligned with fellow *NXT* cast members for a surprise attack on John Cena. Not impressed, the newly formed Nexus banished him from the group. After one day on *Raw*, Daniel Bryan was out of WWE.

Most people would have given up
on their dream or complained.
Daniel Bryan simply worked
harder. He reflected on his
training from Shawn Michaels,
and reminded himself that he
was still a submissions master.
At *SummerSlam* 2010, he received
a second chance and helped Team
WWE defeat the Nexus.

Soon after, he settled his issues
with The Miz. Bryan trapped his
former mentor in his signature
LeBell Lock, winning his first title
in WWE, the United States
Championship. His WWE career
was officially restarted.

Daniel Bryan named his LeBell Lock in honor
of legendary grappler Gene LeBell. It has since
been renamed the "Yes!" Lock and briefly, the
"No!" Lock.

After a heated rivalry with Sheamus over the United States Championship, Daniel Bryan soon found himself reaching higher – 4.6 metres higher, in fact. In July 2011, he outlasted seven other Superstars in the Money in the Bank Ladder Match. His climb to seize the briefcase earned him a World Heavyweight Championship Match whenever he wanted.

Ultimate Underdogs: WWE's Smallest World Heavyweight Champions	
Rey Mysterio	79 kg
Daniel Bryan	**95 kg**
Christian	96 kg
Dolph Ziggler	96 kg
CM Punk	98 kg

Months later, reigning champion Big Show survived a brutal Chairs Match against Mark Henry. Daniel Bryan seized this opportunity. He rushed to the ring to challenge the tired giant. Less than a minute later, Daniel Bryan became World Heavyweight Champion.

With the big gold title around his waist and the  beautiful AJ by his side, Bryan's attitude changed. Though he kept on winning, he was showing signs of overconfidence.

He backed up this new-found
bravado by beating both Big Show
and the equally massive Mark
Henry inside a Steel Cage. Then
he bested five Superstars in the
merciless Elimination Chamber.
The stage was set for *WrestleMania
XXVIII*. Feeling self-assured,
Daniel Bryan headed to WWE's
Grandest Stage to defend his title
against an old foe, Sheamus.

When the moment came, Daniel Bryan completely lost focus. He paused to kiss AJ at ringside, forgetting that the match had officially started. Sheamus took advantage of the distraction. He dropped the smitten Bryan with a Brogue Kick as

soon as he turned round. In just 18 seconds, the "Yes!" Man had lost the World Heavyweight Championship.

The devastating loss could have ended a lesser Superstar's career. Instead, it became a turning point. "Yes! Yes! Yes!" chants became wildly popular with fans, who still believed in Daniel Bryan's abilities. This encouragement boosted his confidence, and the Bearded Warrior kept working towards his goal.

Daniel was soon contending for CM Punk's WWE Championship. However, AJ's head games cost him several opportunities. Their constant lover's spat took an emotional toll. While Bryan, CM Punk, and Kane competed for the title, the devilish Diva toyed with all three combatants. This did not stop Daniel from proposing to AJ.

She accepted, but the quarrelling couple did not live happily ever after. At *Raw*'s 1000th episode, AJ left Daniel Bryan at the altar. Overcome with frustration and heartache, he descended into madness. AJ was appointed *Raw* General Manager, and the torment continued. Soon, Bryan lost control of his temper. He even screamed "No!" in response to supportive "Yes!" chants. AJ forced him to enroll in anger management classes alongside Kane.

The two rivals bickered constantly, to the annoyance of well-meaning counsellor, Dr. Shelby. Despite Shelby's efforts, they could never see eye-to-eye, literally or figuratively.

Forced into a tag team partnership, the duo finally found chemistry.

The arguments never stopped, but with an outlet to channel their anger, they were nearly unstoppable.

Dubbed Team Hell No by the WWE Universe, the odd couple held the WWE Tag Team Championship for an impressive 245 days. They even notched a win at *WrestleMania 29*. It was Bryan's first *WrestleMania* win.

They eventually split up to pursue individual quests, but Team Hell No will be remembered as one of the most dominant and entertaining tag teams in WWE history.

Team Hell No's Greatest Hits

"I am the Tag Team Champions!"
21 September 2012

"Hug it Out"
3 September 2012

A bite to eat
24 September 2012

Anger management graduation
21 January 2013

Legendary Bearded Superstars

Randy Savage

Big John Studd

Hillbilly Jim

Hacksaw Jim Duggan

Back on track in 2013, Daniel Bryan tallied wins over several top Superstars. WWE Champion John Cena believed that Bryan deserved the chance to contend for the WWE Championship. However, certain powerful people disagreed. High atop WWE headquarters, doubt was cast that the "Face of WWE" should be scraggly and rugged.

Facing Cena, the submissions master defied his naysayers. With the crowd at fever pitch, Bryan applied his patented "Yes!" Lock. The Champ powered out of it. Swinging the momentum, Cena attempted an Attitude Adjustment and STF, but the crafty challenger reversed both manoevres.

The stronger Champ turned away Bryan's aerial assault, gaining the edge.

Then, summoning his pent up aggression, Bryan blasted Cena with a running knee, sealing his fate. Confetti rained down from the rafters. The scrappy underdog finally had his moment!

It was short-lived, however. Triple H laid out Bryan with a Pedigree. The treacherous assault allowed Randy Orton to slither to the ring and pin Daniel Bryan, cutting off his WWE title reign at the beginning.

The Authority hand-picked the accomplished Orton as their champion. The Beard and The Viper faced off three times for the title. Each time, interference from the WWE brass prevented Bryan from winning. Even his ex-trainer Shawn Michaels betrayed him with a Superkick. The injustice would not stop.

Despite these numerous setbacks, Daniel Bryan remained as determined as ever. At *Royal Rumble* 2014, he defeated the demonic Bray Wyatt in an instant classic. Fans believed that if the Yes! Man was allowed to enter the Royal Rumble Match, he could have won. Instead, Batista was headed to *WrestleMania*.

At *Elimination Chamber*, The Authority dashed Bryan's *WrestleMania* hopes for the last time. In response, Daniel and his followers took matters into their own hands. The "Yes!" Movement hijacked *Monday Night Raw*! Rabid Beard supporters flooded the ring.

Fans refused to budge until Triple H agreed to face their hero at *WrestleMania*. In a fit of rage, The Game vowed to end Bryan's feel-good story himself at the Show of Shows. Daniel Bryan was on the brink of achieving his dream. Either he or his tormentor would be added to *WrestleMania's* main event.

 The bitter enemies traded vicious blows. Bryan's running knee dropped Triple H for the three-count! However, The Game cut the celebration short, attacking Bryan's injured shoulder.

When the bell rang for the main event, Bryan erased any doubts that he was ready. He endured the pain in his shoulder, and the emotional "Yes!" chants inspired him. He rallied against Orton and Batista.

When The Authority showed up, Orton was trapped in the Yes! Lock!

The evil brass was not done, but neither was Bryan. He flattened them with a flying dive through the ropes. He then hooked Batista in the Yes! Lock, forcing him to submit! The Authority could only watch. The man they dismissed as a "B-plus player" was now the WWE World Heavyweight Champion!

Call him a "goat face" all you want. Daniel Bryan has broken the mould in WWE. He was told he would never make it. Now he is a hero to fans worldwide. No matter what lies ahead, the question of whether Daniel Bryan is ready can be answered with a loud, resounding "YES!"

Daniel Bryan Facts

- Daniel Bryan added to his extensive list of milestones by winning the 2013 Slammy Award for Superstar of the Year.

- Daniel Bryan frequently appears on the hit show *Total Divas* with his wife, WWE Diva Brie Bella.

- Daniel Bryan is a fan of the NFL's Seattle Seahawks.

- On 8 January 2014, Daniel Bryan made national headlines. At half-time during a basketball match against rival Ohio State, Michigan State football players led the capacity crowd in a rousing chant of "Yes! Yes! Yes!" The chant has since become a movement across all sporting events.

STAY FIT, EAT HEALTHY & CHALLENGE YOUR BRAIN
WITH WWE KIDS MAGAZINE

NEW ISSUE ON SALE NOW!

DRINK LOTS OF WATER. STAYING HYDRATED IS THE KEY TO STAYING HEALTHY!

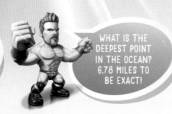
WHAT IS THE DEEPEST POINT IN THE OCEAN? 6.78 MILES TO BE EXACT!

USE YOUR PALM TO MEASURE HOW MUCH LEAN MEAT YOU SHOULD EAT DAILY!

TO SUBSCRIBE GO TO: MAG.WWEKIDS.COM

Index